ROSARIUM

POEMS

HANNAH DOW

CINCINNATI 2018

Acre Books is made possible by the support of the Robert and Adele Schiff Foundation.

ISBN-10 (pbk) 1-946724-09-2 | ISBN-13 (pbk) 978-1-946724-09-0
ISBN-10 (ebook) 1-946724-12-2 | ISBN-13 (ebook) 978-1-946724-12-0

Designed by Barbara Neely Bourgoyne
Cover art: *Abstract Roses* (detail) by Lina Sadziuviene, 2017. Gesso, acrylic, gel ink pen on cotton canvas. 100 x 40 x 1.8 cm (approx. 39 x 16 x 0.7 in).

The press is based at the University of Cincinnati, Department of English and Comparative Literature, McMicken Hall, Room 248, PO Box 210069, Cincinnati, OH, 45221–0069.

Acre Books books may be purchased at a discount for educational use. For information please email business@acre-books.com.

FOR MY PARENTS

I, too, am little more than a stranger in your garden.

—DERRICK AUSTIN, "Vespers"

CONTENTS

ROSARIUM

What Is the Body

if not a nest—
indiscernible like a plover's
shallow hole in sand
lined with shell,
untouchable like a woodpecker's
mine in a tree's soft patch.
If not a verb, a being, the way
a pregnant woman
who arranges her home
in the weeks before delivery
is said to be *nesting*.
How it gathers
everything to itself—
history, windows, warmth.
If not a hive, the bee's boundless
enter and egress,
then a mountain
thought to be a mountain:
what the magma won't miss
when it finally erupts.

Postcard from the Spanish Steps

The artist breathes a divine
varnish, transfigures a body
to burn like sun on new snow.
So like grass to the rain I make him
my god, beg him to fall down
beside me, show me what colors
his hands invent. Everything

disappoints from a lesser
vantage—tempera on wood,
more viscous than it sounds;
that the painting insists on its own
smallness; and the artist's pale body,
slight veins like shadows on his hands.

Halcyon: An Origin Story

After making precise measurements,
a woman travels to the middle of the ocean

to disassemble her ship. She tears the sail
from its mast, strikes from the bottom

as though cutting down a tree, lets it fall.
The hull, she uproots piece by piece by piece,

tosses the fragments overboard. They leap
like fish finding water, bob, bob and float.

Nothing left to stand on, she knots the sail
around her shoulders and, with the pieces,

draws together her nest.

Postcard from the Dead Sea

This is what she wanted—
to be left alone
on the Sea's
placid face,
clutching its fabled
stones to her chest
as if they could grant
her passage to the next
life, as if the fertilizing
salt from the Sea's
own womb could make her
more than mother.
This is what she wanted—
to prove that a person
can drown, become immersed
while still floating, or else
baptized into something more
than water. From the shore
I watch her face sink
from the sun, head
pressed to water
by invisible hands.

Anyone Would Drown

No one saw her emerge from the ocean in midnight darkness, but they awoke to the imprint of her body in sand. Slight curve of the hip said *woman*—said *bird*. Aside from the imprint, no one could prove they had seen her—not when sailors began leaving notes behind that read *I have followed the sound of my love to the sea*. Not when a tidal wave lapped the shore of its trees and its houses, depositing fish skeletons in retreat. Day after day, another swimmer disappeared under a strong current, never to resurface, and still no one could say they had seen her.

Yet she was blamed for all these things. Years later, no one saw a ship collide with the vacant shore. No one saw the sailors, the trees and the houses, the swimmers, disembark. Because they did not see them disembark they did not believe these were their very own fathers, trees, houses, children. They could only believe that a woman had stolen them away with the sound of her voice disguised as wind, as rain, as current, could not understand that a woman and a halcyon had made their home in the same womb.

Postcard from York, Maine

Still, every day like coming to
the ocean in the dark—hearing it,
but only seeing its sudden enormity
upon waking. Your mother's words:
we are not a family anymore.

A gull lands on the seawall. He doesn't feel
the year is new, hasn't checked his body
for changes. He is content to be alone,
or else is learning to live with it.

Home is no protection from even
the smallest storms—
the boarding up of windows,
slight tearing of the sail.

Postcard from Gulfport, Mississippi

One difference between snow

    and march flies? Snow falls,

        the flies' slow drift both

    tumbles and ascends. As I drive,

my windshield gathers only

    the gluey prints of their slight

        bodies, joined in the act of love.

    I find it possible to accept these

        small deaths, to picture

    wings and red thoraxes making

their way toward sky, counting

    descendants as they go.

Genealogy

this tree vines itself to another

like an umbilical cord

like the midwife or its father

forgot to cut it from its mother

and it grew up attached to her

waist without secrets without

rebellion without privacy

what if we were all still joined

Laws of Living

After Spencer Reece

I seal my windows to keep
pests away. Nearby, houses seem
to birth cats, and churches try breathing

assurance into the neighborhood's
decay. High above the immigrant
palm trees, birds navigate a city

of their own. I look at them and feel
the occasional delight I did as a child
while flying in airplanes, my mother

beside me, each of us reading
while the laws of inertia allowed
us to travel at great speeds

without moving our bodies,
without pages turning themselves.
The laws of living bring us to places

we do not plan to go. Places where
flowers bloom all times of year,
where everything closes on Sunday or else

for good. Here, we are promised
Jesus and tomatoes coming soon, promised
a change in season with every vibration

of wings. So when the fig tree disappears from
my yard, the cicadas go with it, but the birds
go on baptizing themselves in their baths.

My father baptized me. My father taught me
to ride a bike. Our first time out on the road
he asked what I should listen for.

Birds, I said, and while he corrected me
gently—such is his way—I have never since
forgotten every given thing I can't control.

Mother, Father, I am trying to make my way
to you, but I have found no laws proving
the logic of a body that journeys without wings.

Variations on *Thank You*

Today, I empty gratitude
from my pockets: butterscotch
wrapper, piece of red string,
and the smooth stone
I leave on your pillow.
And you do not call this *garbage*,
but say I am your crow—
exchanging gifts for the small kindness
that I say is a glimpse of your face.
Sometimes, I think, my thanksgiving
is a hole in the ground—what you don't call
hazard or *nuisance*, but *potential*—
because in the dirty arcs
of my fingernails you see the proof
of something about to ripen.
And in the otherwise silent field
filling with snow, the animals
pushing their dark heads down—
thank you is when I tell you
to watch them pursue
what they know is there,
or was once.

Postcard from Gethsemane

We want grief to be quiet,
something we can hold
all the way up and down
the mountain without letting
on. The trees in this garden
wear grief like they've been
holding it in for a thousand
years, a secret writhing alive
inside that gnarl of trunk, limbs
embracing only themselves.

Why I Will Never Garden

When I was just a wishbone
child I buried lost teeth
between mother's marigolds
and parsley. Because a part
of me had died I willed
the earth to grow me
a sister—bone from my bone.

When a sister never came,
I dug holes across the yard
until the dog refused to walk
outside. I let mother seal
my scrapes with resin,
sat inside and peeled
gluey ghost-prints

from my fingertips. Now,
I refuse the feeling of dirt
beneath my nails, their filthy
arcs reminding me of spades,
of senseless violence
toward the earth, as well as
what's beneath the earth—

root systems that might
tangle around a sister's
ghost-throat. I will never
kneel close to the ground
to hear the voice
that rain makes as it meets
a sun-bathed ground.

Confirmation

When the universe left your womb, the priests
looked to your sister—her set of full teeth,
her oil-black hair, her skin unblemished, unbled.
Limbs like a banyan tree's—open, not inviting.

On your black night, in a voice as clear
as a duck's, she asks: *Did they let you dance?*
Were the goats on fire? Did they wash your hair
with perfume? When they bring me your belongings

how will I know they are yours? You tell her all
you remember is waking into fragrance, into flower
petals torn, into asking for water. The unfamiliar bed,
the unmarked sheets, your thighs soft and heavy, like deer.

In the Garden of Earthly Delights

After Hieronymus Bosch

CENTER

Our bodies are transparent
spheres, amniotic from our birth.
We've learned to crave
the nakedness of a mussel shell,
the stomach round
with extravagant fruit.

LEFT

Feeling taut and unused to my new
skin, the odd bend of my knees, I avoid
your wide gaze. Your eyes are heavy—

sleep or desire? Do you notice how
the rabbits edge around our feet? The single
curve of my breast to hip? And is it you

I am avoiding, or the dragon tree behind
you, the blood I know it holds, and the large-
eyed owl, alert to the uncoiling snake?

RIGHT

A shadow passes over
my body and I feel
the almost ghost

of your touch. But nothing
can save me from knowing
you might be drowning

or tied to a torture
lute where the snake
plays sibilant music. I listen

for your voice, avoid
any surface that promises
to return my gaze.

OUTSIDE

More than half of the body
is water, and meanwhile
all this drought. I would like

to open myself, pour out
from the center and flood,
watch the roots clutch

at the soil like hands
that have just awakened
to their lover's touch.

Reverse Genesis with Drought

The more I asked,
the more you took away.
First, the color green,
so I said

> take the green, but leave
> the flower. Its husk is too
> fragile, even for your hands.

You left me with a fistful of stems,
saying

> see the care with which I hold
> this flower. You call it purple,
> but its infinity is my family.

You promised to return it in abundance.
You took the stream next, and its fish,
too, ladled all into your mouth
as if you'd never eat or drink again.
So I said

> if you take the stream and take
> the fish, then leave the gold,
> the only hope left for this century.

But you said

> you cannot live on gold alone.
> It will disappear from this century
> as soon as I will from the next.

So you left me with my toes in the shallow
bed I began to call my grave.
You remained,
saw the ocean and knew
that it was good. I understood
your devastating greed,
said

if you take the ocean you will die
of thirst. If you take the ocean,
you will wrench the moon from its perch.
And you said
foolish child, if I unhang
the moon I will undo everything
I have done these last three days.
And you drowned me in a darkness
punctured not even by white stars.

Postcard from Caye Caulker, Belize

I saw you from the airplane:
small light. I held my book
to you and read. On the page,

I found the letters of your name
and spelled you until the words
burst open like seed pods and

scattered you around my feet.
How fragile you are in my hands.
How well I know you, to know

what black spores you hold
and what happens when
you're split and buried, left alone.

Infinitely Yours

Let's crash a party, I'll be your plus-one.
You'll wear your tie and I'll wear my dress.
We'll poach leftovers from the funeral crowd—
muffins, macaroni salad, finger
sandwiches—we'll take
flowers from the tombs and tie

them through our hair. Loosen your tie,
let's be going now, on to the next one—
a penthouse somewhere, we'll take
the elevator to the highest floor, undress
the sky with our eyes, dance beneath the finger-
moon, away from all the crowds.

Next, we'll crash a wedding, crowd
around an altar and watch two strangers tie
the knot, put rings on their fingers,
promise: *you're the only one.*
And when she, in her white dress,
and he, whose eyes see only her, take

off in their shiny car, we'll take
balloons from chairs, drinks from a crowded
bar—flutes of champagne dressed
up in bubbles—something to tie
us over for infinity: plus one, plus one,
plus one. Lacing my fingers

through your expectant fingers,
let's watch the prom king take
his queen around the dance floor, one

more song before the crowds
disperse and they're alone. Now tie
me to your sail and we'll address

our next adventure: a dressage
competition, where your trained fingers
will hold me like a rider whose hands are tied
to reins, walk me around the arena, take
me in pirouette before the crowd.
Bow. Applause. And just one

more thing—let them take
our picture before the world crowds
in, before we're one plus many ones.

Not My Day

I am at another wedding
not my own, feeling like
I'm as important enough to be
here as the carpet's fringe—
a nice addition, if pointless

and occasionally in the way.
I'm in a new dress, but Jesus
is the only one who knows it,
and not just because he saw me
cut off the tags and slide it over

my head this morning, but
because he stares at me
while everyone else looks
to the altar, where the action
happens, though I wouldn't call it

that—for all their hype and eternal
implications, ceremonies feel so
uneventful. *Do you mind
sharing your limelight?* I ask
Jesus, because no one but me

notices him or the way
his muscles thrust
in chiseled pain. The priest
says something about bodies—
how two become one,

and I imagine bride &
groom joined at the hip,
like the plastic couple
perched this very moment
on their three tier vanilla cake,

and the pain of being
irreversible, altered this way.
Jesus says this wedding
was his idea. He likes bringing
people together, likes parties,

and says the wedding of two
bodies is pretty much the same
altering thing that happens
when I let him inside of me.
So I married Jesus—

I should have predicted this
when I first walked down
that aisle—he hasn't taken his eyes
off me yet, and it's not even my day.
Do I think he'll make a good

husband? Not if I'm the jealous
type. I don't think I'll like
the way he loves everyone equally
or watches every woman in the world
undress before slipping into bed.

The World Is Throwing Me a Surprise Party

The trees are in on it, too.
They wave until I notice
how well they've bloomed
into party outfits, how they've
changed in public. They're not shy.
Neither are the morning birds
who practice *happy birthday*
when they think I'm still asleep.
The mailman passes by my house,
saving up my cards—he'll throw them
like confetti when I open the door.
My friends do not return my calls.
They act like they don't know me,
afraid they'll ruin the surprise.
And my husband is gone
on business for a month, time
enough to find me perfect gifts—
red Italian wines, a Japanese harp,
perfume scraped from a rose's hip.
The moon, if he could. But it
has a prior engagement—
it's been practicing its brightness,
stretching its broad face
a little more each night,
and tomorrow, I will sway
beneath the fullness.

Advice from a Marriage Counselor

It is easier to love a body crouched over a toilet, vomiting, than one summoning dust and the greenness of age. Your partner, when dead, will still ignore your demands that he cut his fingernails or mow the lawn or flush the toilet, and once you have died, you will no longer hear the flushing of toilets, so you might as well get used to it. When you are dead, it no longer matters who you wake up next to or whether you are laughing or if he can make a good lemon meringue pie. And you must not forget that after a mere twenty years, children begin to raise themselves. Because when it comes to marriage, what matters most is whose name appears adjacent to yours on a tombstone and whether you will agree on an epitaph, because what is written in stone is written in stone.

Please Don't Feed the Spirit Animals

I saw a pair of mechanical polar bears
getting it on at the Vienna Prater. It was
unexpected—his bucking her from behind

while I slid by unobserved in a no-rail
cart. Knees to my chin, bar low and tight
across my lap, I dropped the fake

camera I'd been instructed to use.
They were polar bears in everything
but spirit, I decided—or else all spirit,

no polar bear. I couldn't know. Who
signed them up for this? Were these
exhibitionists in another life, banished

to a special circle of pseudo-Arctic hell?
Or was this a celibate's reward? Sex in heaven,
perpetual love-making, no threat of offspring.

A giant crab looked on from across the way.
And how was he supposed to feel,
lit up only by his own fluorescence?

Our Lady of the Jail

A man and a woman were out shopping for a jail.

I would like a dormitory-style jail, said the man. I want to sleep on bunk beds and, when the feeling arises, pretend I am on a sinking ship.

I would prefer a panopticon-style jail, said the woman. I want to feel I am always the center of attention.

I think there is a way to accommodate both your wishes, said the realtor. Look here, this jail was once underwater. And looters visit so frequently, you will not forget you are being watched.

A once-submerged jail would make the sinking ship game more riveting, said the man.

And I do love being watched, said the woman. Even while I am getting undressed . . .

Will you take it? said the realtor, who began to lock them inside before they could respond.

Postcard from Los Angeles, California

You were always fond of anything
that could melt, and so I found you

at the bottom of my cocktail glass
where you were hiding beneath a smile

of orange, a globe of ice. On the bus,
I witnessed you Cubist: a man modeling

your scars—another, your small tuft
of above-the-collar chest hair.

I looked outside the window and saw
your face in the O of a Taco Bell,

your bike locked up outside
the hair salon—the bike that left

grease stains on my palms. I looked down
at my palms, saw roses, winced

at the open-close of their tender blooming.
How down to earth you are. What certainty

I have in knowing where to look for you—
you, certain as the world, as a traffic light,

quickly changing when I blink.

Variations on *Goodbye*

Sometimes, my goodbye assumes
it will see you again—in a café, staining
a teacup with your lips, or home
in your underwear, frying eggs.

My goodbye, like an old man serving
beer, like snot in a tissue, like a flag
at half-mast, tells it like it is. It says: *watch me
crest this wave, man.* Flirtatious, it twirls

hair around its long, slender fingers,
pops gum between its glossy
teeth. Sometimes, it expects not
to see you again. It is the average

finger in the air. A finger prepared
to press a button. Once it was a kiss
ripening on your hand. Now it is
the stone fruit's pit, just before

the toss. Or the hand on a ship's
wheel, a petticoat swelling with
the wind, while the shark makes
its long descent, realizes latitudes.

The Harp Knows How To Be Stripped Bare

After Duchamp

And the fish knows how to be stripped bare.
And the bed. Each feels in the strumming

of its ribs the call for a missing part. A loss
less obvious than death. Like pocket change.

Like drought. Like learning how to not grow
old, as in uncapping the fountain of youth

and casting vapors on the world. So the harp
never buzzes, the fish never grays, the bed never

folds into itself. So the harp lives forever
on a stage. The fish, on a chopping block. The bed,

on display in an empty room. And when the sun presses
its thick body against a nearby window—drown

the lights, pull the shades. Let them sing sad music,
make love to the silence. Allow, at least, this modesty.

Liturgy

Whenever you do this,
you say, bowing

and raising my legs
to eye level, left hand

ceremonious
behind my back *(in memory*

of me) be pleased
(with the sacrifice
I am making). How

the body, like a church,
is a crime scene—

the evidence of which
you can wash

from your hands,
from your mouth.

You tell me to eat
what is holy—*Take this*
(and eat, this is my body).

How my body, like a church,
like a crime scene, isn't holy:

it is the overturned chair,
slow-burning flame—

do (this in memory of)
me—the evidence of blood

without the stain. It takes
everything to keep
its integrity intact.

Origin of Salt

A man and a woman build a house of stones.
They do not build a roof because it never rains.
After two days, they say, what shall we drink?
The water, says the woman.
But the lake is so beautiful, says the man, we should not disturb it.
We will die without it. She makes a cup with her hands and drinks.
He makes a cup with his hands and drinks.
After several years, the lake has retreated many inches.
The man, the woman, and their child must walk out very far to cup
    their hands and drink.
What can we do? says the woman. We will run out of water.
We can make our cups smaller.
The man makes a cup with his child's hands, saying, see? Now we
    will live many more years.
After many more years, the child's hands are as large as his father's.
What can we do now?
We must conserve, says the woman. We must separate our tears
    from their salt.

Imitation

All at once, the plants began
to die. Trees surrendered leaves
in late summer, coneflowers
curled black and in on themselves,
and the rose hips never ripened.
The grass brittled and browned,
hedges hummed when the wind
rattled their skeleton limbs.

Inside, I removed floral: yanked
curtains from their rods like weeds,
unstitched every tiny blossom on blouse
or handkerchief. I drew fresh coats
of *Aged Barrel* across the walls, set fire
to the potted plants and counterfeit
flowers, watched them blaze,
saw how flattering it was.

Postcard from Yosemite

Let the black trees say there is more fire
here than water. Sequoias, like snakes, need

the kind of shedding only a good burn
can provide. This is the way water transpires,

becomes flame—from the ground up
to the tops of trees, spreading the way

the sun deposits light, or climbs down
rocks as if for the first time leaving

some long-dormant volcano, learns, like
any idea, to tumble over itself, ablaze.

Postcard from the Salton Sea

If the rain came now, it would flood the cobblestone
patterns of dirt where the lake should be. And the ground
would not know what to do, unable to bury all this water
inside itself. If the rain came now, dead fish would blanket
its surface as the lake rebuilt itself. And the fish would be
washed clean of the dust they have worn like a shroud
for months. If the rain came now, it would entomb the canoe
that rests in the middle of the lake. And the bodies
in the canoe would appear to earthmovers of the next drought.

Poem with Inexact Apocalypse

How far we'll go

for eggshell powder

swirled into a water glass:

some of us build strength

like homes—from the bones

up. We will know the time

has come when dogs cease

to lick our wounds, to dig

our holes, leave us for

the forests' clay, bury

their game in the marlstone

of unsoiled plains.

Updates on the Drought

I

Gills on the brink
of collapse, you learned
breath with your hands—
dug sand from your chest
with the hard gift of shell,
carved space for the parching
air. Your lungs bloomed
at first gasp, before
the withering of your face,
the disappearance of scales.

II

When the sun jaundiced
the white curtains, your skin
cracked into geometric
shapes, subtle hair faded
to brown. And as your feet
uprooted from the foot
of the bed—you felt the sudden
need to be covered, to wrap
your body in the thin
shroud of flowers
wilting behind your ears.

III

You begged the sky
for rain, but it sent the fires
instead, like gods with plaster
skin and wicking eyes,
thundering through a storm
of flames. All the thirst
that it created, sent to drown
you in your own blistering.

IV

Rather than bones, the ocean
deposited salt in your vanishing.

Our Lady of Arts & Crafts

The handkerchief in her pocket, initials
almost yours. She embroidered them
herself, first attempt at the seed stitch,
so *K* looks more like *H*. If she had known
you'd go so soon she would have buried
you in the backyard alongside tomato plants
with a tag to track your progress, to ensure
that you would thrive, drowned you
in resin like an insect or a flower, fastened
you around her neck on a chain whose clasp
requires extra hands, another body, to undo.

The Crowning

Look in my garden,
don't you see yourself

haunting the ladyslippers,

the grass that brushes
your feet? This is the way

to imagine you: ceramic

and standing as if
some angel has just left

a crown of sunlight

on your head. Sometimes
I come here to thread the vowel

of our names together: Hail,

woman of candles, daughter
of fables, mother of trawl.

Hail the blade-shaped leaves,

clay beneath a vacant grave.
See the snow shroud as it falls,

note the indifference of hail.

0

After Dorothy Wordsworth

Some things stay—

rain, orchids, moonlight—

same. All morning, my mind

a rising hummingbird. Rain like blinking
wind. And I cannot forget the way
mild night keeps the weather

from this illness,
walks us to our graves.

Postcard from Grasmere, England

I press my forehead to the floor
and ask forgiveness for poor
listening. A dove rests in the crown
of birch limbs on my head. I've grown
holier these moments I've spent
with my legs folded and bent
like a grasshopper's, singing
as he sings, chafing
all parts together. A duck cleaves
the lake's smooth surface and leaves
me wishing I could do anything
      so precisely.

Options for Penance

Fill your living room with flowers. Keep the cat from poisonous ones.

Write the Our Father in chalk. Write it one hundred times. When you finish, erase everything and write it all again.

Lie naked in the snow. Be washed clean.

When your hand bleeds, do nothing to stop it. The body mends itself.

Put on your wedding dress. Climb out the upstairs window, stand on the roof. People will mistake you for the Virgin Mary, build shrines in your honor, light candles across your yard.

Put salt on your wounds instead of your food.

Lock yourself in a room with roses. Kneel before them until they die, until their scent disappears from your hair. Whichever comes first.

Variations on *I'm Sorry*

The apology I give you is shaped
like an egg. When it cracks, I let it
drain from hands to arms, follow

my veins like the rivers they are.
My apology is fast-moving, knows
where it's going and when it will

arrive. And it arrives. My apology
knows how to make an entrance.
It dazzles in its fur coat and sapphires.

Everyone turns their heads to look
at my apology as it goes, lips slightly
parted. See me mouth the words

to my apology—ripe and firm.
Don't be alarmed by the powder
it leaves on my tongue, the bees flying

in and out of my mouth. We all
need something sweet, something
gold and worth blossoming for.

Postcard from Kansas City, Missouri

Little known fact: this is the capital
of dead baby birds. No one knows
how or why, from where they fall.
We step cautiously around the gray-
pink of them and their large sealed eyes
without considering how a bird falling
resembles a miscarriage—*spontaneous*
loss—or that the name Phoebe means
bright, but also *small passerine bird*,
but also *sister, daughter, girl*, or how
anything that dies before seeing is
born into darkness, swaddled in cries.

Postcard from Kansas City, Kansas

This city is this city on both sides
of the state line, the way grass is green,
et cetera—yet for all the arguments
a border can cause, this one has always
felt invisible to me. Even birth,
a kind of border, a crossing into,
carries its own dim edges: we only know
the moment we lost you, that you passed
into life without living, no grand Persephone
moment, no eyes adjusting to the sun.

Echolocation

Last night I dreamt of wings. I dreamt that you
did not use words but rather echoed sounds
I could not hear, in a pulse I could not feel. Beloved:

if I had found a way to make you see
that I was not your prey, you could have searched
for me the way you forage nectar and
forestalled the sequent deafening you felt.

Photographs after a Murder: Memphis, 1968

At the scene
a custodian pushes
blood into jars
with a broom.

Briefcase quiet
folded pajamas
shaving cream set
to leave in the morning.

Woman on a balcony
mourning. Wants God.
Answers. To plunge toward
another derelict building.

A ghost in this one
or blurred man
walking. Agnostic
photographer says

man, blames an eye
that blinks too slowly,
as if resurrected
photographs were not
some embryonic ghosts.

Postcard from the Kunsthistorisches, Vienna

In early depictions, Jesus carries his cross
like it's made of feathers, without breaking
a sweat. Not until the late Middle Ages,
I learn, did artists think to emphasize
his burden: a heavy line in sand, fine
red attention to strokes along his crown,
bound wrists, neck yanked like a dog's—

all to make me feel something like devotion.
Yet I cannot imagine myself in his place
or swoon like a Boschian virgin. I do not
see a face that resembles my own in the hostile
crowd. I only feel that I've swallowed something
small and alive—a bird whose wings
keep gravity from drawing me to my knees.

What to Make of the Shape of Your Body in the Bed

—its obsolescence the kind that sheds
its leaves come fall, loses what warmth

it should be gaining. A little like the way
I say your name each morning,

a ritual I wish into prayer, wish into
your wristwatch's easy wandering—

yet feel its indifference move
from hand to hand like winter's

repetition, impossible to hold.

A Dream of Burial Means to Acknowledge Something in Your Life Is Ending

For Raechel

When the heart clenches
like a willful child, the body falls
to the pavement it has long
loved. We are not deer,

stumbling into light, but we
chase, and we chase, and we chase.
Some say we remember how to live
when we remember we are dying—

still, we press heel to dirt,
the open wound, and we turn
and we promise we will see you
at the end. What, besides gravity,

keeps us here? We too could collapse
into the earth's diurnal mouth, could
learn the end is always promised, or
learn to descend and yet blossom.

Self-Portrait with Dragonfly

After Mary Szybist

She looks at me with so many eyes
invisible to mine.
Twice-winged and aching

to break into
a new skin, much
like you are undressing now—
shedding the shirt, wilted
with sweat, that smells of summer
pavement rain.

*

We have migrated across oceans
in tandem, our heavy bodies

conspicuous in flight.

*

I am doubled now.
Beside myself
when you take me

by the back of the head,
bend me into a shape
we find suitable.

See how much our body is
like a circle.

Does this pose make us look eternal?

ACKNOWLEDGMENTS

I would like to thank the editors of the following publications where variations of these poems first appeared:

American Literary Review: "The Harp Knows How to Be Stripped Bare"

Armchair/Shotgun: "Confirmation"

The Carolina Quarterly: "Postcard from the Kunsthistorisches, Vienna," "Postcard from the Dead Sea," "Postcard from Yosemite," "Postcard from York, Maine"

The Cincinnati Review: "Variations on *I'm Sorry*"

Crab Orchard Review: "Not My Day"

Cumberland River Review: "Our Lady of Arts & Crafts"

fields: "Why I Will Never Garden"

Harpur Palate: "Our Lady of the Jail"

Hawai'i Pacific Review: "Origin of Salt"

The Journal: "Postcard from Gethsemane," "Self-Portrait with Dragonfly"

The Keats Letter Project: "Postcard from the Spanish Steps"

The Louisville Review: "Postcard from Kansas City, Missouri," "Postcard from Gulfport, Mississippi"

Lumina: "Imitation"

Minetta Review: "Photographs after a Murder: Memphis, 1968"

Ninth Letter: "Postcard from Grasmere, England"

North American Review: "What Is the Body"

Rock & Sling: "Postcard from the Salton Sea"

Slush Pile Magazine: "Advice from a Marriage Counselor," "Echolocation"

Soundings East: "Halcyon: An Origin Story," "Options for Penance"

Spoon River Poetry Review: "The World is Throwing Me a Surprise Party"

Switchback: "Reverse Genesis with Drought"

The Open Bar at *Tin House*: "Please Don't Feed the Spirit Animals"

Whiskey Island: "Postcard from Los Angeles, California"

"The Harp Knows How to Be Stripped Bare" was the Verse Daily: Web Weekly Feature on August 1, 2016. "Infinitely Yours" and "Postcard from Los Angeles, California" each won an honorable mention in the 2015 and 2017 AWP Intro Journals Awards. "Imitation" was reprinted in the anthology *The Absence of Something Specified* (Fern Rock Falls Press, Noah's Shoes Press, Tiger's Eye Press, Uttered Chaos). Several of the poems here also appeared in my chapbook, *Options for Penance*, published by dancing girl press (2017).

I wish to thank my friends, mentors, and colleagues at the University of Pennsylvania, Loyola Marymount University, the University of Southern Mississippi's Center for Writers, and the University of California–Irvine, especially Gregory Djanikian, as well as my generous and discerning first readers: Brandi George, Martina Sciolino, and Emily Stanback. Special thanks to Angela Ball and Rebecca Morgan Frank, whose wisdom, generosity, and encouragement have been unparalleled. To Amy Gerstler and Michael Ryan: deepest gratitude for allowing me the valuable time, space, and support to be a poet. Thank you to the marvelous editors at Acre Books, Danielle Cadena Deulen and Nicola Mason, for making this journey a delight. And to Joe, my dear friends, my family: infinite appreciation to you for making me, and this book, possible.

NOTES

The line "We want grief to be quiet" in "Postcard from Gethsemane" is a rewrite of the first line of Mary Szybist's poem "Crylight."

In "Why I Will Never Garden," "wishbone child" is derived from a phrase in Mary Karr's memoir, *The Liar's Club*.

Some details in "Confirmation" were inspired by stories of living goddesses, or kumaris, worshipped by Hindus and Buddhists in Nepal. Kumaris are young girls who live cloistered until puberty, when they relinquish their powers to a new living goddess.

The italicized words in "Liturgy" are phrases from the Catholic mass.

"Photographs after a Murder: Memphis, 1968" is an ekphrastic poem written after photographs taken by Joseph Louw and published online in *Time Magazine*, April 3, 2015.